CARS

IAN GRAHAM

A⁺

Smart Apple Media

Published by Smart Apple Media
2140 Howard Drive West, North Mankato, Minnesota 56003

Created by Q2A Creative, Editor: Chester Fisher, Designers: Mini Dhawan, Ashita Murgai
Picture Researcher: Ankita Kilawala

Printed in United States

Library of Congress Cataloging-in-Publication Data
Graham, Ian, 1953-
Cars / by Ian Graham
p. cm. — (Mighty machines)
Includes index.
ISBN-13: 978-1-58340-917-6
1. Automobiles—Juvenile literature. I. Title. II. Series.

TL147.G66 2006
629.222—dc22   2006002930

2 4 6 8 9 7 5 3

CONTENTS

MIGHTY CARS

Cars have completely changed the modern world. They give people great freedom to travel wherever they want to go and to cover long distances very quickly.

Small car

Sports car

The United States is home to a third of the world's cars.

TYPES OF CARS

There are lots of different types of cars. Small cars are good for short journeys and are easier to park in small spaces. Sedans are more comfortable for long journeys. Hatchbacks have a rear door. Sports cars are small, fast cars that are fun to drive. Off-road vehicles, or "four-by-fours," travel well over muddy, rough ground. Modern supercars are amazingly expensive, fast cars. The mightiest cars of all are racecars, dragsters, and jet cars, which have set speed records.

○ Many different types of cars are built suitable for a wide range of driving conditions.

Sedan

Four-by-four

THE NUMBERS GAME

Cars are more popular than ever. There are about 600 million cars on the world's roads today, and about 40 million new cars are built every year. There are so many cars that the traffic in big cities often slows to a walking pace or grinds to a halt altogether. This is called a gridlock.

FAST FACTS
Right or Left
Three-quarters of the world's cars are driven on the right side of the road. Britain, Ireland, Japan, Australia, and New Zealand are places where cars drive on the left.

○ New cars are shipped around the world and delivered by special transporters.

5

HOW CARS WORK

Cars are made in different shapes and sizes, but most of them work in the same way. A car is a set of systems that work together.

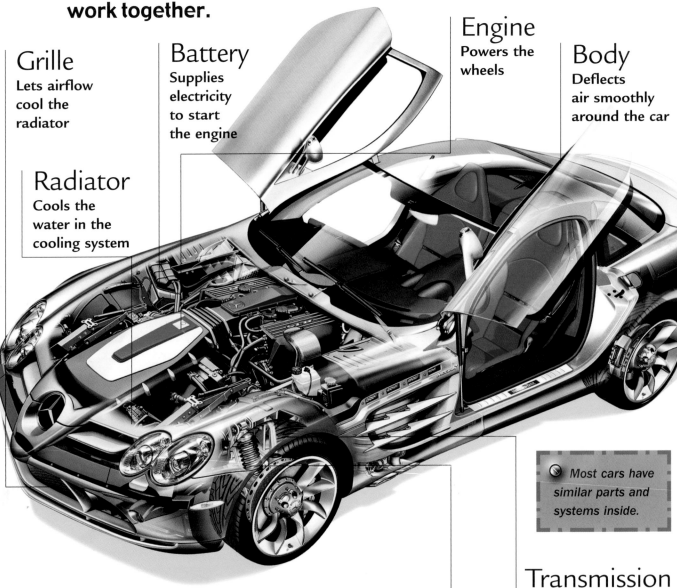

Grille
Lets airflow cool the radiator

Battery
Supplies electricity to start the engine

Radiator
Cools the water in the cooling system

Engine
Powers the wheels

Body
Deflects air smoothly around the car

Most cars have similar parts and systems inside.

Transmission
Connects the engine to the wheels

Suspension
Gives a smooth ride on bumpy ground

HOW A CAR WORKS

The fuel system supplies fuel to the engine. The electrical system makes electricity for the engine, lights, radio, and other electrical parts. The lubrication system keeps the engine's moving parts covered with slippery oil. The engine drives the wheels.

INTAKE ┄┄► **COMPRESSION** ┄┄► **IGNITION** ┄┄► **EXHAUST**

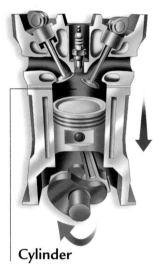

Cylinder

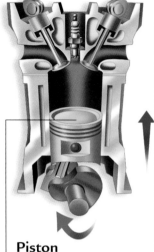

Piston

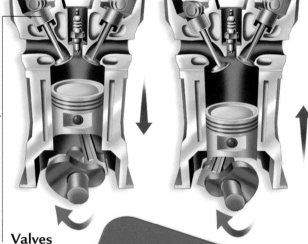

Valves

How valves work
Valves at the end of each cylinder are designed to open and close at exactly the right moment to let fuel in and waste gases out.

INSIDE A CAR ENGINE

A car engine works by burning fuel inside tubes called cylinders. Most car engines have four, six, or eight cylinders. When fuel burns inside a cylinder, the heat makes air in the cylinder expand. The force of expanding air pushes a piston down the cylinder. Pistons moving up and down inside the cylinders provide the power to turn the car's wheels.

FAST FACTS
Waste Products

When a car's engine burns fuel, it produces hot gases. The exhaust system lets these hot gases escape and also makes the engine quieter. In many cars today, the exhaust system cleans up harmful gases before they escape into the air.

THE FIRST CARS

The first road vehicle that moved under its own power was a three-wheeled army tractor built more than 230 years ago.

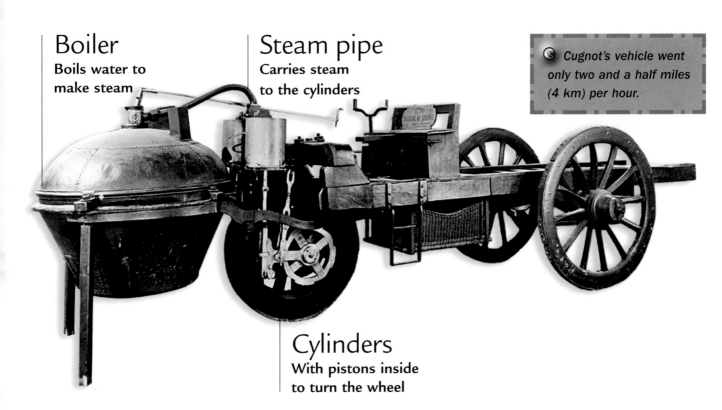

Boiler
Boils water to make steam

Steam pipe
Carries steam to the cylinders

Cugnot's vehicle went only two and a half miles (4 km) per hour.

Cylinders
With pistons inside to turn the wheel

STEAM POWER

In 1769, a French soldier named Nicolas-Joseph Cugnot built a strange-looking vehicle. It was a three-wheeler with a steam engine. A boiler at the front was filled with water. A fire heated the water and changed it into steam. The steam worked the engine, which turned the front wheel. It could only travel at a walking pace, but it showed everyone that road vehicles could move under their own power.

Steam made in the boiler moved pistons up and down inside two cylinders. The pistons turned the front wheel.

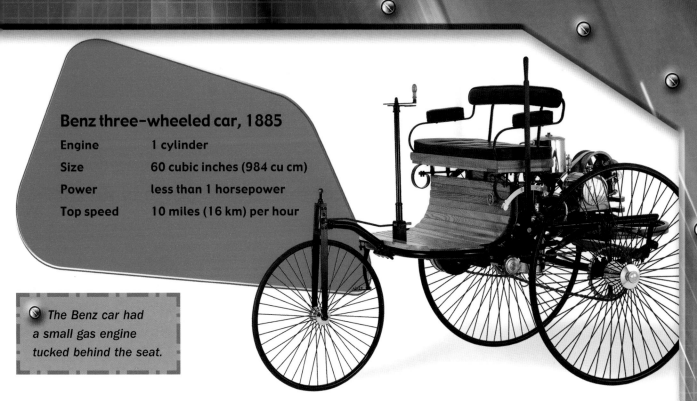

Benz three-wheeled car, 1885

Engine	1 cylinder
Size	60 cubic inches (984 cu cm)
Power	less than 1 horsepower
Top speed	10 miles (16 km) per hour

The Benz car had a small gas engine tucked behind the seat.

FROM STEAM TO GAS

In 1885, a German engineer named Karl Benz built a new type of car. Its engine worked by burning gas instead of making steam. It was the first motor car. Steam cars couldn't move until they made enough steam, but gas cars could get going as soon as their engine started, and they didn't need a big boiler full of water.

In 1886, Gottlieb Daimler installed a gas engine on a coach and produced the first four-wheeled car.

Tires
Pneumatic (air-filled) from the 1890s

9

CARS FOR ALL

The first cars were very expensive. Only rich people could afford to buy one. But some car makers set out to build cars that everyone could afford to own.

MODEL T

Henry Ford believed that people wanted simple cars that didn't cost much. He was right. In 1908, Ford began making the Model T. In the first year, he sold 10,000—an amazing number for that time. Over the next 19 years, more than 15 million were produced. The Model T became the most popular car in the world.

Roof
Folds down to the back

Windshield
Folds down

Wheels
Made of wood, with pneumatic (air-filled) tires

Henry Ford's Model T cost $825 when it went on sale in 1908. By 1926, the price had fallen to only $290.

Body
Available in different styles

Engine
20 horsepower

Starting handle
Turned to start the engine

Engine
In the rear

Luggage
Carried at the front

BEETLES AND MINIS

In the 1930s, Ferdinand Porsche designed a simple "people's car," or Volkswagen, in Germany. It became known as the Beetle because of its shape. More than 21 million Beetles were made. When the Mini Cooper appeared in 1959, people were surprised at how tiny it was. However, Minis became so popular that they are still being made today.

FAST FACTS

Front-wheel Drive
The Mini's engine powered the front wheels. This was very unusual for the 1950s.

The new Mini Cooper is an updated version of the hugely popular original Mini.

BF54 WNE

SUPERCARS

Most cars are made in large numbers to reduce the cost of each one so that more people can buy them. But some cars are designed to be the best, no matter what the cost. These amazing cars are sometimes called supercars.

BUGATTI VEYRON

The Veyron is the fastest, most powerful, and most expensive production car. Its amazing engine and body shape give it a top speed of about 250 miles (400 km) per hour. As the car speeds up, a wing rises up from the back to keep it steady on the road. A car designed for such high speeds needs special tires. Its back tires are the widest of any road car's.

Step 1. The rear wing tilts up.

Step 2. The wing rises at higher speeds.

Air scoops
Let in air to cool the brakes

Snorkels
Let air into the engine

Tires
Created specially for the Veyron

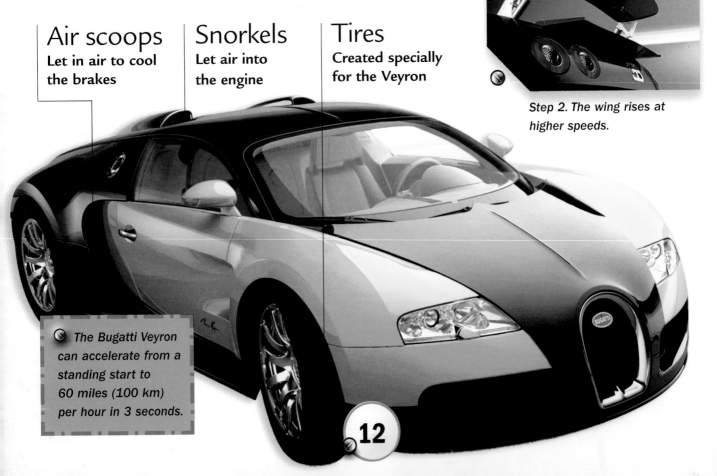

The Bugatti Veyron can accelerate from a standing start to 60 miles (100 km) per hour in 3 seconds.

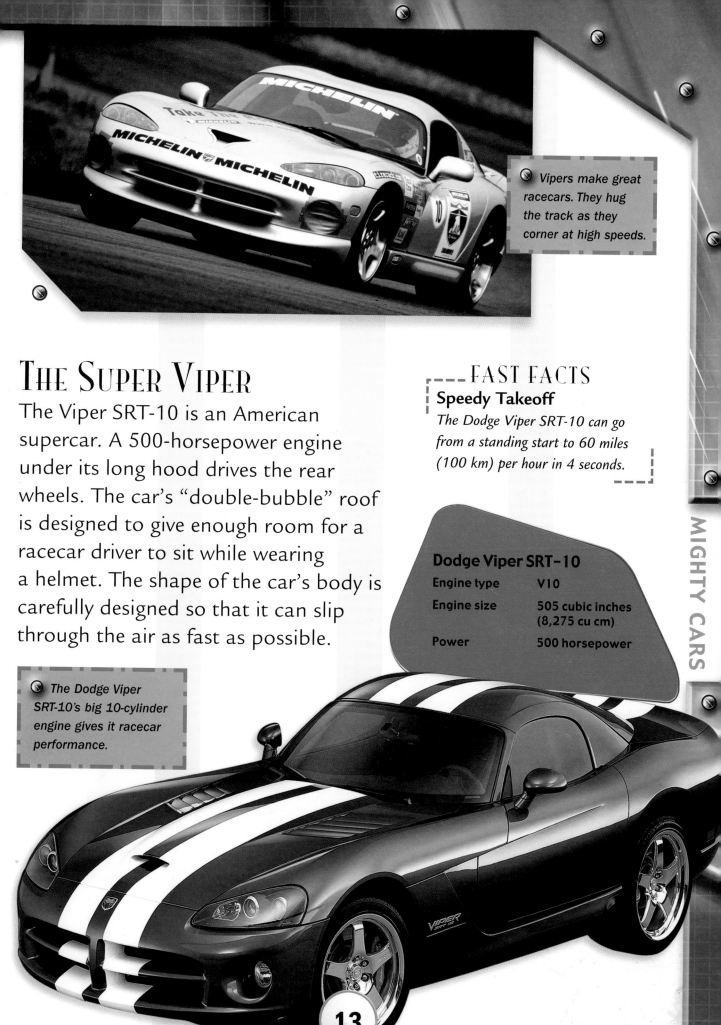

Vipers make great racecars. They hug the track as they corner at high speeds.

THE SUPER VIPER

The Viper SRT-10 is an American supercar. A 500-horsepower engine under its long hood drives the rear wheels. The car's "double-bubble" roof is designed to give enough room for a racecar driver to sit while wearing a helmet. The shape of the car's body is carefully designed so that it can slip through the air as fast as possible.

The Dodge Viper SRT-10's big 10-cylinder engine gives it racecar performance.

FAST FACTS

Speedy Takeoff
The Dodge Viper SRT-10 can go from a standing start to 60 miles (100 km) per hour in 4 seconds.

Dodge Viper SRT-10

Engine type	V10
Engine size	505 cubic inches (8,275 cu cm)
Power	500 horsepower

MAKING CARS

Cars used to be built by people, but robots have now taken over a lot of the work. A modern car factory can build a car in less than 20 hours.

PUTTING IT ALL TOGETHER

In the first car factories, each car stayed in one place while workers built it. Henry Ford changed to a faster method. Chains pulled the cars through the factory, and workers installed parts as the cars passed. Moving assembly lines are still used in car factories, but today many of the workers are robots.

Moving assembly line
To speed up car production

There were few machines on early car production lines. Most of the work was done by hand.

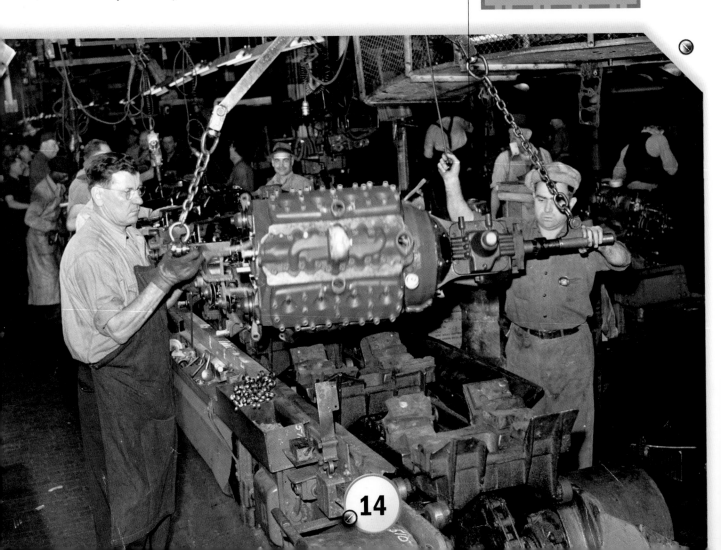

Robots that build cars can use different tools, including mechanical hands to pick things up, drills to cut holes, spray guns for painting, and welding tools to join pieces of metal together.

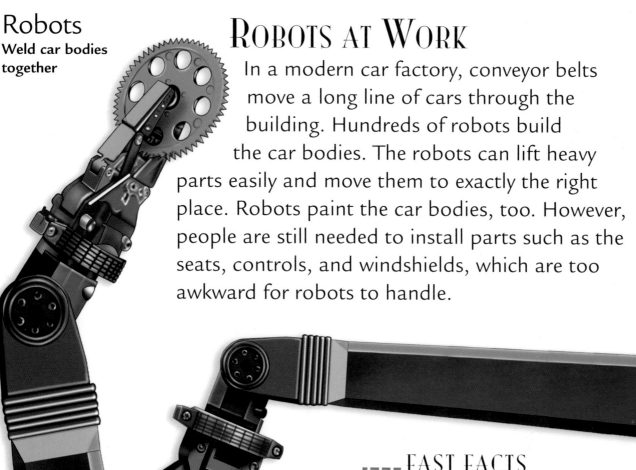

Robots
Weld car bodies together

ROBOTS AT WORK

In a modern car factory, conveyor belts move a long line of cars through the building. Hundreds of robots build the car bodies. The robots can lift heavy parts easily and move them to exactly the right place. Robots paint the car bodies, too. However, people are still needed to install parts such as the seats, controls, and windshields, which are too awkward for robots to handle.

FAST FACTS
Robot Car Workers

Nearly half of all the robots in the world work in factories helping to make cars.

15

RACECARS

Autoracing is one of the most exciting and popular sports. The fastest racecars thunder around racetracks at up to 250 miles (400 km) per hour.

SINGLE SEATERS

Formula 1 cars, Champ cars, and Indy Racing League cars are all single-seat racecars. They are just big enough for the driver to wriggle down inside. Their wings work like upside-down aircraft wings. They press the car down and make its tires grip the track better so that it can corner faster.

Formula 1 racecar	
Engine type	V10
Engine size	183 cubic inches (3,000 cu cm)
Power	860 horsepower

Tires
Made of a soft rubber for maximum grip

Cockpit
The driver's compartment

Engine
Drives the back wheels

Rear wing
Presses the rear wheels down

Body
Made from carbon fiber

Front wing
Pushes the car's nose down

A Formula 1 racecar is built by hand. Each car contains about 10,000 parts.

BURNING UP THE STRIP

Dragsters are cars designed to go as fast as possible down a straight quarter-mile (400 m) track called a drag strip. Top Fuel Dragsters are the fastest. They accelerate away from the starting line faster than a fighter plane or a Formula 1 racecar. They cross the finish line at nearly 335 miles (540 km) per hour. A whole race may last less than five seconds!

> The secret of a Top Fuel Dragster's amazing speed is its 7,000-horsepower engine, as powerful as 8 Formula 1 racecars!

FAST FACTS
NASCAR Racing
American NASCAR racecars look like ordinary cars, but each is a hand-built racecar with a top speed of 200 miles (320 km) per hour.

CARS AT WORK

Police cars are packed with equipment to help police officers do their work. The inside of a modern police car can look more like an office than a car!

POLICE CARS

A standard police car today not only carries a radio, but it also has a computer and video equipment. The crew uses all of this equipment to contact other officers, check if other cars have been stolen, and even measure the speed of other cars. While a car's speed is checked, a video camera records its picture, and its details are downloaded into the police car's computer.

Light bar
Warns drivers that a police car is approaching

Body
A standard production car body

Police cars are filled with computer and communications equipment.

Grille
May conceal video camera and radar speed detector

Computer
Displays information about crimes

Radio
Lets the crew talk to other officers

CARS AT WAR

Wherever American soldiers go, their Humvees go, too. The Humvee, or High Mobility Multipurpose Wheeled Vehicle (HMMWV), is a small truck, but soldiers use it like a car to get around because it's a tough vehicle with enough room inside for four fully equipped soldiers.

A police car driver is surrounded by buttons and switches that control all of the extra equipment the car carries.

FAST FACTS
Electric Cars
The first police cars in the 1890s were powered by electricity because there were very few cars with gas engines.

The Humvee has lots of space underneath so that it can travel over rough ground.

CUSTOM CARS

Most cars are built in large numbers, and each car is the same as thousands of others. Some people want their cars to be different from other cars. Making a car different is called customizing, and the cars are called custom cars.

Hot Rods

All custom cars are designed to look cool. Some are designed to be powerful and fast, too. These custom cars are called hot rods. Most custom cars begin as a family car. The car's shape is changed, a new engine put in, and an eye-catching design painted on.

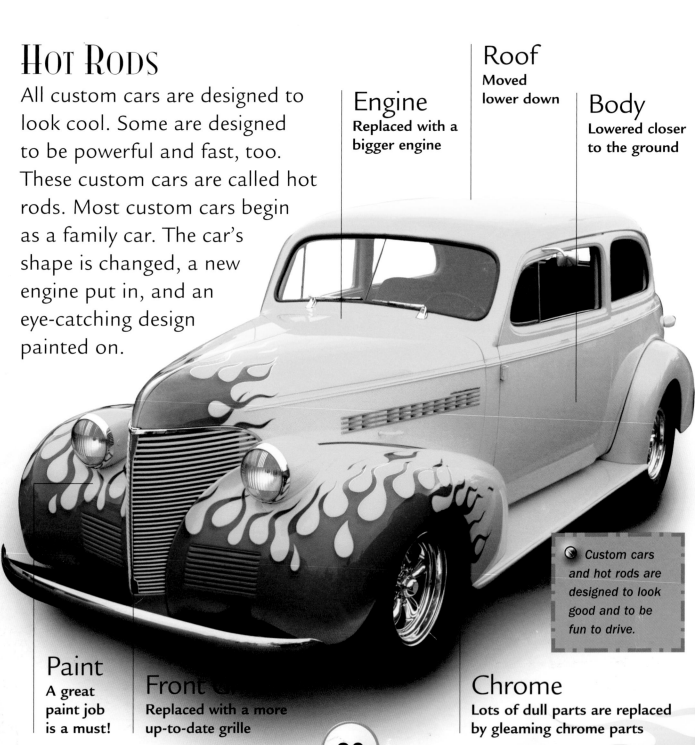

Engine
Replaced with a bigger engine

Roof
Moved lower down

Body
Lowered closer to the ground

Paint
A great paint job is a must!

Front G...
Replaced with a more up-to-date grille

Chrome
Lots of dull parts are replaced by gleaming chrome parts

Custom cars and hot rods are designed to look good and to be fun to drive.

Stretch limos are luxurious inside. There's plenty of room for big, comfortable seats, television sets, DVD players, and sound systems.

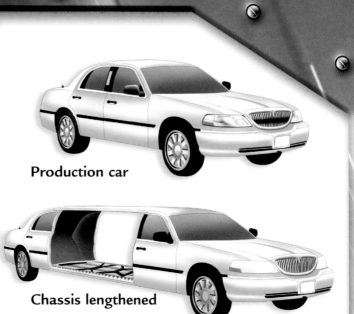

Production car

Chassis lengthened

Structure strengthened

Body rebuilt

STRETCH LIMOS

An extreme way to customize a car is to cut it in half and make it longer. The front and back of the car are pulled apart, and an extra section is put in the middle. The finished car can be up to 10 feet (3 m) longer! A car customized like this is called a stretch limousine, or stretch limo. Stretch limos are used for special trips or events.

A stretch limo needs a super-strong chassis, or frame, underneath to keep it from sagging in the middle!

FAST FACTS

History of Flame Painting

Flame painting first started in California in the late 1940s. Today, subtle flames, screaming flames, and tribal and traditional flames are a popular part of hot rods.

VIP SPECIALS

Presidents, royalty, and other very important people (VIPs) often travel in large luxury cars. However, these are not ordinary luxury vehicles. These cars are specially built to protect their passengers from attack.

ARMORED CARS

The cars that carry the most important people have an armored body and bullet-proof glass to protect against gunfire and small bombs. The window glass can be more than two and a half inches (6.4 cm) thick! The engine is armored, too, so that the driver can keep the car moving and drive away from danger.

The U.S. President travels in safety in a Cadillac deVille with top-secret armor and other special defenses.

Run-flat tires
Work even with holes in them

Satellite tracker
Finds the car if it is stolen or hijacked

Night vision
Lets the driver see in the dark

Body
Lined with bullet-proof armor

Windows
Made from bullet-proof glass

Fuel tank
Stops the fuel from exploding

An armored limousine undergoes a fiery test.

TESTING TIME

The makers of armored cars know how well they work because they test the cars. No other cars are put through tests as tough as this. Armored cars are tested by being shot at and blown up to make sure that they really do protect their important passengers!

FAST FACTS

Gas Attack!

The most expensive armored VIP cars have airtight doors and windows to protect the driver and passengers against chemical and biological attacks.

23

MODERN CARS

Cars have changed a lot since the Benz three-wheeler in 1885. Modern cars are bigger, heavier, more powerful, faster, more comfortable, more reliable, and safer, too.

SAFETY FIRST

Modern cars are safer than old cars because they are thoroughly tested. They are deliberately crashed to check how strong they are. Special mechanical people, called crash test dummies, sit in the cars to show what would happen to real people in a crash.

Crash tests
Check how strong cars are

Crash testing makes sure that cars are strong enough to protect people inside and shows any weak spots in a car.

Instruments
Send information to computers

Damage
Filmed by high-speed cameras

> A car's air bag bursts out at up to 200 miles (320 km) per hour. This is so that it's fully inflated before the driver's head hits the steering wheel.

BUCKLE UP!

Modern cars have lots of safety features and electronic aids. Antilock brakes stop cars quickly without skidding. Seat belts hold the driver and passengers tightly in their seats. Air bags blow up to cushion the impact of a crash. Satellite navigation systems help drivers find their way.

FAST FACTS

Crash testing cars began in the U.S. in the 1950s. It was soon being used in many other countries by car manufacturers.

> A car's navigation system figures out exactly where the car is by receiving radio signals from satellites in space.

RECORD BREAKERS

The fastest cars in the world have jet engines! They are cars built to set the fastest of all the car speed records—the land speed record.

Faster Than Sound

On October 15, 1997, a car called *Thrust SSC* crossed the Black Rock Desert in Nevada faster than a jumbo jet airliner! SSC stands for supersonic car, because *Thrust SSC* was designed to go faster than the speed of sound.

Engines
Two Rolls-Royce Spey 205 jet engines

Thrust SSC is as powerful as about 116 Formula 1 racecars!

Parachutes
Help to stop the car

Cockpit
Houses the driver, fighter pilot Andy Green

Wheels
Made from solid aluminum

Chassis
Frame made from welded steel tubes

Nose cone
Sharp to punch through the air

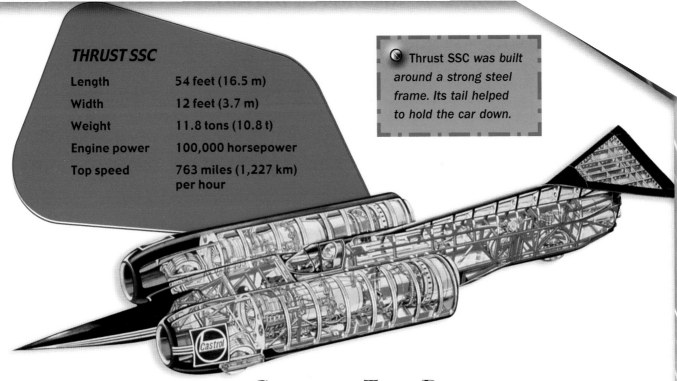

THRUST SSC

Length	54 feet (16.5 m)
Width	12 feet (3.7 m)
Weight	11.8 tons (10.8 t)
Engine power	100,000 horsepower
Top speed	763 miles (1,227 km) per hour

Thrust SSC *was built around a strong steel frame. Its tail helped to hold the car down.*

SETTING THE RECORD

To set the record, *Thrust SSC* had to drive along a course in the desert faster than the speed of sound, then turn around and do it again in the opposite direction, all within one hour! A car going as fast as *Thrust SSC* is not easy to stop. Brakes alone won't work. *Thrust SSC* shot parachutes out behind it to help slow it down.

Spirit of America—Sonic Arrow *challenged* Thrust SSC *for the land speed record in 1997. Its driver, Craig Breedlove, sat in the car's nose in front of a fighter plane's jet engine.*

FUTURE CARS

Future cars will probably be kinder to the environment. They will have cleaner engines or no engines at all. Some of them may even be able to fly.

FLYING CARS

Movies set in the future sometimes show cars that can fly. Well, some flying cars have already been built! The Moller Skycar is powered by four pods with fans inside. The fans are driven by eight engines. The jets of air from the fans can be sent in different directions to steer the car in the air.

> ⊗ *The Skycar's engines burn the same gas that cars use, so the Skycar can land at an ordinary gas station to fill up.*

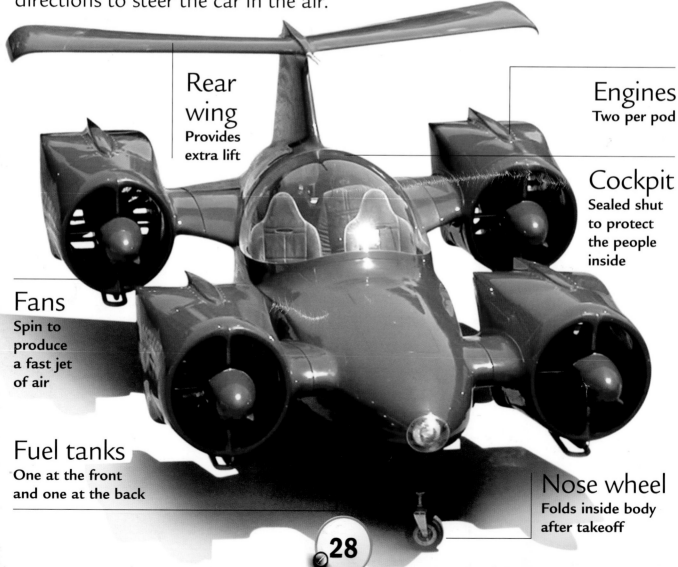

Rear wing
Provides extra lift

Engines
Two per pod

Cockpit
Sealed shut to protect the people inside

Fans
Spin to produce a fast jet of air

Fuel tanks
One at the front and one at the back

Nose wheel
Folds inside body after takeoff

This is where the fuel cell is.

Cars like the General Motors Hy-Wire cut air pollution because their fuel cells are cleaner than car engines today.

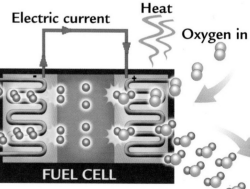

Electric current

Heat

Oxygen in

Hydrogen in

FUEL CELL

Water out

FUEL CELLS

Some future cars may have no engine! Instead, they might be powered by fuel cells. A fuel cell is a device that makes electricity from chemicals. Fuel cells are being used by some spacecraft, and fuel-cell cars have already been built. The General Motors Hy-Wire is a fuel-cell car.

FAST FACTS
Shuttle Power
The space shuttle uses fuel cells to make electricity and drinking water.

TIMELINE

BF54 WNE

1769
The first self-propelled vehicle is built by Nicolas Cugnot.

1865
The Red Flag Act forces British drivers to have a man walking in front of their vehicle waving a red flag for safety!

1885
Karl Benz builds the first successful motor car.

1886
Gottlieb Daimler designs the first modern gas engine.

1893
Benz builds his first four-wheeled car.

1893
The first car license plates are introduced in France.

1896
Electric cars are introduced.

1898
The first land speed record, 39 miles (63 km) per hour, is set by an electric car.

1899
The world's first self-propelled police vehicle, an electric car, is used in Akron, Ohio.

1904
The first taxis are equipped with a meter for measuring distance and speed.

1908
The Ford Model T is introduced.

1910
The first police motor car, a Model T Ford, starts work in Akron, Ohio.

1916
More than half of the world's cars are Model T Fords.

1916
Cars with windshield wipers are introduced in the U.S.

1927
The last Model T Ford is produced.

1938
The Volkswagen Beetle is introduced.

1951
Chrysler introduces power steering in cars.

1959
The Mini Cooper is introduced.

1962
The first robots are installed in a car factory in the U.S.

1997
First supersonic land speed record set by *Thrust SSC*.

1998
The VW New Beetle is introduced.

2002
There are more than 530 million cars in the world.

2003
The last of the original VW Beetles is manufactured.

2003
Drivers have to pay to bring their cars into central London.

GLOSSARY

assembly line

The part of a car factory where cars are put together.

crash test dummy

A mechanical model of a person used for car safety tests.

cylinder

A space inside an engine that a piston moves in and out of. Burning fuel pushes the piston out, making the engine work.

exhaust

The gases that come out of an engine when fuel is burned.

fuel

A liquid, such as gas, burned in a car engine to provide the energy to turn the car's wheels.

hatchback

A car with an extra door in the back.

horsepower

A unit used to measure the power of a car's engine. A small car might have an engine of about 100 horsepower.

hot rod

A customized car that has been rebuilt and repainted to be fast, good-looking, and fun to drive.

lubrication

Covering the moving parts of a car's engine with oil so that they slide over each other easily.

off-road vehicle

A car designed to work well on soft, muddy ground. Also called a four-by-four because all four of its wheels are driven by the engine.

radiator

Part of a car's engine that cools the water or oil inside it by letting air blow around it and carry the heat away.

sports car

A small car designed to be fast, sleek, and fun to drive.

stretch limo

A luxury car that has been rebuilt with an extra section in the middle to make it longer.

supercar

A very expensive, powerful, and fast car.

suspension

A system of springs and other parts that allows a car's wheels to move up and down over bumps.

transmission

The gears and other parts of a car that connect the engine to the wheels.

V8

A popular type of car engine. It has eight cylinders in two rows of four, connected together at the bottom to make the shape of a letter V.

INDEX

WEB FINDER

http://suzy.co.nz/suzysworld/Factpage.asp?FactSheet=256 *Car facts, experiments, and jokes!*

http://www.nhra.com/streetlegal/whatisadragrace.html *Find out about drag racing.*

http://www.nhra.com/streetlegal/funfacts.html *Lots of fun facts about drag racing.*

http://www.scapca.org/cool_car_facts.asp *Cool facts about cars with cleaner engines.*

http://www.indyracing.com/indycar/garage/facts.php *Lots of fun facts about auto racing.*

http://www.howstuffworks.com/nascar *Find out about NASCAR racecars.*

http://www.wsc.org.au *Visit this Web site to learn about racecars powered by sunshine!*

http://www.guinnessworldrecords.com *Use this Web site to find out about record-breaking cars.*